# QUICK AND EASY COOKING

## Tasty, Healthy, Complete Meal Planner

Cheryl Thomas Peters, D.T.R.

REVIEW AND HERALD® PUBLISHING ASSOCIATION
HAGERSTOWN, MD 21740

This book was
Designed by Bill Kirstein
Photography by Meylan Thoresen*
Type set: 12/15 Goudy Old Style

PRINTED IN U.S.A.

99 98 97 96          10 9 8 7 6 5

**R & H Cataloging Service**

Peters, Cheryl Thomas, 1962-
    Quick and easy cooking: tasty, healthy complete meal planner.
    1. Cookery. 2. Cookery—Vegetables. I. Title.
        641.5636

ISBN 0-8280-0445-5

*Full-color photographs of actual meals prepared by the author
using the ingredients outlined in the menus.

# TABLE OF CONTENTS

# DEDICATION

I dedicate this book
to my mother,
who taught me the joys
of healthy living, wholesome meals,
and entertaining.

# FOREWORD

"These intriguing menus contain nutritional ideas that give a fresh approach to the dullness and drudgery of low-cholesterol and low-fat cooking. Not only do they represent the latest recommendations of the American Heart Association, but they also include the high-fiber, high-complex carbohydrate features that are equally as important in preventing heart disease.

"Most Americans eat too much fat and start it at too early an age. The potential appeal that these menus carry to teens and young adults, encourages the formation of low-fat eating habits that will carry into adulthood—a much-needed trend.

"If one were to incorporate the author's cooking principles into regular practice, the reduction of heart events, strokes, and hypertension would be gratifying. This collection has great promise for those searching for creative cooking ideas that are both healthful and interesting. Let us have more!"

Dr. R. L. Hoenes, M.D.
Internal Medicine/Cardiopulmonary Disease
Sonoro, California


"This book helps bridge an important gap in nutritional science.

"There are many books written on nutrition for persons with heart and great vessel disease who are looking for a strict therapeutic diet.

"There are also a number of books written for persons who are interested in eating generally well-balanced meals and who have no physical problems.

"The particular appeal of this volume is that it combines the best of general nutrition without liberalism with the best of therapeutic nutrition without fanaticism.

"In short, it is a well-written, well-balanced preventative nutrition book that can guide whole families into nutritious, balanced, sensible, tasty, and health-promoting eating practices."

Dr. Richard L. Neil, M.D., M.P.H.
Program Director for Health Promotion and Education
School of Public Health
Loma Linda University

# Goals of This Book

The goal of this book is to provide nutritionally balanced, complete menus designed for the prevention of heart disease, obesity, and cancer. To achieve this goal, the following guidelines have been followed in each menu:

● Through the use of plant foods, each menu meets the United States recommended daily allowance for protein.

● Menus contain decreased amounts of cholesterol and fat through observing the following limitations:

   ○ No more than one-half egg per serving.

   ○ Oil and margarine are used in place of shortening and butter to increase polyunsaturated fats and decrease saturated fats and cholesterol. (Note: When margarine is called for, use margarine that contains a liquid corn oil as its first ingredient rather than a hydrogenated oil. This will further decrease the intake of saturated fats and increase polyunsaturated fats.)

   ○ Olive oil contains lower amounts of saturated fat and higher amounts of polyunsaturated fats than other oils. However, its taste becomes strong upon heating, so you may prefer to use it primarily for cooking in strong-flavored recipes.

● Sodium amounts are based on approximately 3 grams per day.

● Menus feature low-sugar, low-calorie desserts.

● Recipes contain increased levels of dietary fiber.

● Variations are given in many recipes that enable the cook to lower fat and sodium amounts. Also given are replacements for dairy products. (Note: For those following the therapeutic low fat, low cholesterol, or low sodium, be sure to delete sodium, oils, and margarine when stated in recipe as "optional" or "to taste," and use the smallest amount when options are offered [e.g., ½ to ¾ cup, use the ½ cup]. Nutrient information is based on low-fat variations, and optional ingredients are not included in the nutrient calculations.)

# INTRODUCTION

This book is ready to help you plan 24 complete meals, all of them nutritionally balanced. They are quick to prepare, often taking less than an hour from the time you walk into the kitchen to the time you call the family to the table. Not only do the meals make life easy for the cook, but they have the simple elegance that is fitting for special occasions and entertaining.

The greatest advantage of this meal planner over other cookbooks is its harmony with the recommendations made by the American Heart Association and the American Cancer Society. Cholesterol, saturated fats, salt, and sugar have been cut to the minimum. It also follows their recommendations to increase dietary intake of fruits, vegetables, and grains in order to prevent heart disease and cancer.

Because all the recipes succeed without meat, some people may wonder if the meals provide enough protein. Texas Christian University computer-analyzed each recipe to discover what percentage it contains of the U. S. recommended daily allowance for protein and other nutrients. The author included the results in this book to assure you that your family will get the protein, vitamins, and minerals they need in each meal.

The publishers thank you for purchasing this book and trust that it will enhance the health of you and your family.

# BREAKFAST

- Hearty Country Breakfast
- Sunrise Breakfast
- Skier's Breakfast
- Breakfast in New England
- Breakfast With a Citrus Surprise
- Continental Breakfast
- All-Time-Favorite Family Breakfast

NOTE: If following a therapeutic diet, please read Goals of This Book before continuing with the recipes.

# HEARTY COUNTRY BREAKFAST

**Country Gravy Over Whole Wheat Toast**
**Coconut Fruit Medley**
**Cranacot Drink**

## COUNTRY GRAVY

(Serves 4-6)

¼ cup margarine
3½ tbsp. flour
2½ cups skim milk*
¼ cup Baco chips
2-3 eggs (optional)†
¼ tsp. garlic powder or
    to taste
½ tsp. salt (optional or
    to taste)

1. Hard-boil 3 eggs.
2. In large skillet, melt margarine over medium heat.
3. Add flour 1 tablespoon at a time, whisking with wire whip after each addition until smooth.
4. Add milk one cup at a time, whisking with each addition until smooth. If too thick, add a little more milk as needed.
5. Add Baco chips, sliced hard-boiled eggs, and seasoning. Let gravy simmer, being careful to not let it boil, until Baco chips are softened.
6. Serve immediately over biscuits or toast. (See Whole-Wheat Bread recipe, p. 51.)

\* May use any milk substitute—almond milk, soy milk, etc.
  See recipes in last chapter under variation recipes.
† If eggs are included, this recipe contains one-half egg per serving.

# COCONUT FRUIT MEDLEY

(Serves 4)

1 cup pineapple chunks, drained (save juice)
1 large banana, sliced
2 medium oranges, peeled and cut into chunks
½ cup moist, flaked coconut

1. Pour pineapple juice over banana slices; drain.
2. Lightly toss all ingredients.
3. Chill until served.
4. Garnish with sprigs of mint or fresh fruit.

Variations: Just before serving, add fresh or frozen blueberries, peaches, grapes, melon, raspberries, or strawberries.

# CRANACOT DRINK

2 cups cranberry juice, chilled
2 cups apricot nectar, chilled

(Serves 6)
1. Mix juices. Serve.
Makes 4 cups.

NUTRITIONAL ANALYSIS FOR MENU

| | |
|---|---|
| Calories | 667 |
| Protein | 18g |
| U.S. RDA | 39% |
| Carbohydrate | 96g |
| Fat | 25.3g |
| Cholesterol | 34mg |
| Sodium | 614mg |

# SUNRISE BREAKFAST

**Granola With Milk**
**Whole-Wheat Toast With Apricot Butter**
**Grapefruit Cup**
**Hot Herbal Tea**

## GRANOLA

(Serves 22)

7 cups oatmeal
1¼ cups wheat germ
1¼ cups coconut
½ cup brown sugar (add more or less to taste)
2 tsp. vanilla
⅔ cup water
½ cup oil
1 cup chopped nuts (almonds, walnuts, pecans)
½ cup dates, chopped (optional)
1 tsp. salt (optional)

1. Mix dry ingredients in gallon-size bowl.
2. Combine liquid ingredients in separate bowl, mixing well.
3. Slowly add liquid mixture to dry ingredients, mixing thoroughly with each addition.
4. Spread thinly on four large cookie sheets and bake at 250° to 300° F for 1½ hours, mixing after each half hour. Add dates, raisins, or dried apricots, etc., and bake an additional half hour.
5. Remove from oven and cool. Store in airtight container. Makes 11 cups.

# APRICOT BUTTER

(Serves 24)

2 cups dried apricots
1 cup frozen apple juice
    concentrate
2 tsp. vanilla (optional)
1 tsp. grated orange rind
    (optional)
¼ tsp. salt, or more

1. Soak apricots several hours in the apple juice concentrate until fruit is soft; drain and save liquid.
2. Whiz apricots in blender with remaining ingredients, using only enough of the liquid to operate blender.
3. Use as a spread for toast.

Makes 1½ cups.

# GRAPEFRUIT CUP

2 grapefruit
1 pint strawberries
¼ cup sugar

(Serves 4)

1. Cut grapefruit into halves.
2. Cut around edges and membranes to remove grapefruit sections. Place sections in bowl.
3. Remove membranes from grapefruit shells and reserve shells.
4. Cut strawberries into halves and place in bowl with grapefruit sections.
5. Sprinkle sugar over fruit. Toss. Cover and refrigerate.
6. Just before serving, fill grapefruit shells with fruit mixture. Garnish with mint leaves if desired.

NUTRITIONAL ANALYSIS FOR MENU

Calories.................................................................................481
Fat .....................................................................................13.1g
Protein .................................................................................14.5g
    U.S. RDA ........................................................................32%
Cholesterol ..............................................................................2.5mg
Sodium .................................................................................340.5mg
Carbohydrate.............................................................................81.3g

# SKIER'S BREAKFAST

**Whole-Grain Cereal**
**Applesauce or Milk***
**Blueberries**
**Slivered Almonds**
**Whole Wheat Toast With Raspberry Jam**
**Roma Hot Drink or Postum**

## WHOLE-GRAIN CEREAL IN CROCKPOT

(Serves 6-8)

½  cup oatmeal (long-cooking)
¼  cup cornmeal
¼  cup millet†
¼  cup rye flakes
¼  cup barley
¼  cup wheatberries†
¼  cup (or to taste) dried apricots, sliced
¼  cup dates, sliced
 4  cups water

1. In a crockpot, mix all ingredients the night before. Use ¼ cup each of your favorite nuts, grains, or seeds, totaling approximately 2 cups. Add your favorite dried fruit, using more or less, depending on sweetness desired.
2. Add water in ratio of 2 to 1 with dried ingredients, i.e., 4 cups of water to 2 cups of dried ingredients.
3. Cook on low 6 to 8 hours. For longer cooking time, add 1 more cup water to prevent cereal being too dry. Add more or less water for consistency desired. I enjoy mine moist so I am liberal with the water.
4. Serve with milk* or applesauce. Garnish with blueberries and slivered almonds, or your favorite fresh fruit.

Makes approximately 6 to 7 cups.

\* May use any milk substitute—almond milk, soy milk, etc. See recipes in last chapters under Variation recipes.
† Available at local grocery store or health food store.

# RASPBERRY JAM

**(Serves 18)**

1⅛ cups apple juice
2½ tbsp. cornstarch
1⅛ cups raspberries
½ tbsp. honey
⅛ tsp. lemon juice

1. In saucepan, dissolve cornstarch in chilled apple juice. Bring mixture to a boil and continue to boil for 1 minute over medium heat, stirring constantly.
2. Add remaining ingredients. Add more honey for desired sweetness.
3. Cook 30 seconds. Chill.
4. Serve as spread for whole-wheat toast.
Makes 2¼ cups.

# KAFFREE ROMA,* OR POSTUM HOT DRINK

Enjoy an all-natural caffein-free instant beverage with a rich and satisfying coffee-like flavor, made from roasted grains.

These beverages are available in many local grocery stores. If not available, check with a health food store or an Adventist Book Center. Many of these stores will order this for you if they do not carry the product.

*Brand name

---

**NUTRITIONAL ANALYSIS FOR MENU**

| | |
|---|---|
| Calories | 433 |
| Fat | 6.2g |
| Protein | 13.5g |
| U.S. RDA | 29% |
| Cholesterol | 0 mg |
| Sodium | 217.7mg |
| Carbohydrate | 85g |

# BREAKFAST IN NEW ENGLAND

New England Vegetable Breakfast
Cottage Cheese Delight
Whole-Wheat Bread
Tomato Juice With Lemon Wedge

## NEW ENGLAND VEGETABLE BREAKFAST

6-8 potatoes, halved
3-4 carrots, sliced
1 medium onion, sliced
2-3 cups frozen peas
¼- ½ head cabbage, quartered
and thinly sliced
Margarine to taste
Salt to taste

½ cup low-fat cottage
cheese
1 tomato slice
1 leaf of lettuce

(Serves 4)
1. In medium-size saucepan, layer vegetables in order.
2. Lightly steam vegetables in small amount of water until tender.
3. Serve each vegetable separately on plate.
4. Top with margarine and salt. This looks so simple, yet it is so flavorful with all the vegetables steamed together.

## COTTAGE CHEESE DELIGHT

(Serves 1)
1. Place lettuce leaf on a salad plate. Top with tomato.
2. Use ice-cream scoop to place cottage cheese on tomato. Garnish with green onion, onion slices, or paprika.

NUTRITIONAL ANALYSIS FOR MENU

Calories ................................................. 537
Fat............................................................ 4.5g
Protein..................................................... 34.8g
  U.S. RDA............................................... 76%
Cholesterol ............................................. 9.5mg
Sodium .................................................... 1170 mg
Carbohydrate........................................... 3.1g

# BREAKFAST WITH A CITRUS SURPRISE

**Kiwi and Orange Toast**
**Oatmeal Raisin Muffins**
**Banana-Mango Smoothie**

## KIWI AND ORANGE TOAST

3 kiwis, peeled and wedged

3 oranges, peeled, sliced into circles

2¾ cups pineapple juice

3 tbsp. cornstarch

¼ tsp. salt

¼ tsp. cold water

8 slices of toast

1 cup fresh berries to garnish

(Serves 8)

1. Slice kiwis into wedges.
2. Slice oranges into circles.
3. Heat pineapple juice to boiling.
4. Mix cornstarch, salt, cold water. Add to boiling juice and cook 5 minutes, stirring constantly.
5. Add kiwis and orange slices and cook 3 minutes or just to heat through.
6. Serve over toast. Garnish with fresh strawberries or blueberries.

# OATMEAL RAISIN MUFFINS

**(Serves 12)**

2 eggs,* separated

⅔ cup skim milk†

⅓ cup oil

1 cup oatmeal

1 cup flour

2 tsp. baking soda**
   (optional)

⅓ cup sugar or 3 tbsp.
   molasses

2 tsp. cinnamon

½ cup raisins or
   currants

1. Mix egg yolk (one yolk discarded), milk, and oil.
2. Stir in oatmeal, flour, soda, sugar, cinnamon, and raisins or currants.
3. Beat egg whites until stiff, but not dry; quickly and carefully fold into batter.
4. Spray muffin tins with Pam or lightly grease. Bake at 400° F for 20 minutes. Let cool and store in airtight container. (Muffins freeze well.)

* This recipe contains one-eighth egg per serving.
† May use any milk substitute—almond milk, soy milk, etc.
See recipes in last chapter under variation recipes.
** Baking soda may be omitted in this recipe. However, muffins will not be as light without it.

# BANANA-MANGO SMOOTHIE

**(Serves 6)**

1 cup ripe mango, chopped

1 cup fresh pineapple chunks

1 medium banana, cut into fourths

1 cup skim milk*

1 cup low-fat yogurt*

2 tbsp. honey

1 tsp. lime juice

½ tsp. vanilla extract

1. Combine all ingredients in blender; process until smooth.
2. Chill thoroughly.

Makes 4½ cups.

\* May use any milk substitute—almond milk, soy milk, etc.
See recipes in last chapter under variation recipes.

### NUTRITIONAL ANALYSIS FOR MENU

Calories.................................................................................456
Fat.....................................................................................8.9g
Protein ..............................................................................11.2g
    U.S. RDA ........................................................................24%
Cholesterol ........................................................................4.7mg
Sodium.............................................................................365mg
Carbohydrate.......................................................................85.5g

# CONTINENTAL BREAKFAST

**Cranapple-Nut Muffins**
**Whipped Cranberry Butter**
**Fresh Pineapple Wedges**
**Orange Juice**

## CRANAPPLE-NUT MUFFINS

2 eggs,* separated
1 cup skim milk†
⅓ cup vegetable oil
1 medium apple, pared and chopped
¼ cup unsweetened applesauce
1 cup cranberries, chopped or halved
⅓ cup brown sugar or 3 tbsp. molasses
1 tsp. cinnamon
½ tsp. salt
2 cups whole-wheat flour
2 tsp. baking soda** (optional)
½- ¾ cup chopped nuts

(Serves 12)

1. Heat oven to 350° F. Spray 12 medium-sized muffin tins with Pam or lightly grease.
2. Mix 1 egg yolk (one yolk discarded), milk, oil, apple, applesauce, and cranberries.
3. Stir in flour, soda, brown sugar, salt, and cinnamon until flour is moistened. Batter will be lumpy.
4. Beat egg whites until stiff, but not dry; quickly and carefully fold into batter.
5. Add ½ cup nuts to batter.
6. Fill muffin cups about three-fourths full. Sprinkle remaining chopped nuts on top of each muffin.
7. Bake 12 to 15 minutes or until golden brown. Immediately remove from pan. These muffins freeze well.

MICROWAVE REHEAT DIRECTIONS:

| Muffins | Room Temperature | Frozen |
|---|---|---|
| 1 | 10-15 seconds | 20-25 seconds |
| 2 | 20-30 seconds | 35-40 seconds |
| 4 | 30-35 seconds | 55-60 seconds |

* This recipe contains one-eighth egg per serving.
† May use any milk substitute—almond milk, soy milk, etc. See recipes in last chapter under variation recipes.
** Baking soda may be omitted in this recipe. However, muffins will not be as light without it.

# WHIPPED CRANBERRY BUTTER

½ cup very soft mar-
    garine
½ cup fresh cranberries,*
    finely chopped
    or canned whole cran-
    berry sauce

*Sugar to taste

(Serves 16)
1. Wash and drain fresh cranberries.
2. Whip soft margarine with mixer until very light and fluffy.
3. Fold in chopped cranberries. Use as a spread on warm muffins.

Makes 1 cup.

# FRESH PINEAPPLE WEDGES

1. Cut off both ends of fresh pineapple. Use medium-sized sharp knife to cut off outer shell, going around the pineapple, cutting from top to bottom. (May also halve pineapple and peel.) Cut out eyes if desired.
2. Sprinkle generously with salt and rub into pineapple to reduce acid. Rinse thoroughly under cold water to remove salt.
3. Slice and serve in wedges.

NUTRITIONAL ANALYSIS FOR MENU

| | |
|---|---|
| Calories | 359 |
| Fat | 17.5g |
| Protein | 7.14g |
| U.S. RDA | 15.5% |
| Cholesterol | 22.2mg |
| Sodium | 288mg |
| Carbohydrate | 46g |

# ALL-TIME-FAVORITE FAMILY BREAKFAST

**Silver Dollar Blueberry-Banana Pancake Clusters**
**Peach Sauce Topping** ◆ **Applesauce Topping**
**Banana Slices** ◆ **Peanut Butter**
**Orange Circles** ◆ **Milk†**

## SILVER DOLLAR BLUEBERRY-BANANA PANCAKE CLUSTERS

(Serves 6)

2 eggs,* separated
½ cup quick-cooking oats
½ cup whole-wheat flour
2 tsp. baking soda** (optional)
¾ cup milk†
2 tbsp. vegetable oil
1 tbsp. honey
½ tsp. salt
½ cup fresh or frozen blueberries
1 medium banana cut in ¼-inch pieces.

1. Beat oats, flour, soda, milk, oil, and honey until smooth. For thinner pancakes, stir in additional ¼ cup milk.
2. Add salt to egg whites; beat until stiff; gently and quickly fold in egg yolks and add to above batter.
3. Fold in blueberries and bananas.
4. Spray nonstick fry pan with Pam or lightly oil and heat pan to medium heat.
5. Pour approximately 2 tablespoons batter (enough to make 2-inch diameter pancakes) into hot pan. Cook until puffed and bubbly with dry edges. Turn and cook other side until golden brown.
6. To keep pancakes hot, stack on hot plate with paper towels in between, place on cookie sheet in warm oven, or rewarm in microwave briefly to prevent toughness.
7. Top pancakes with peanut butter, peach sauce topping (recipe following), or applesauce and top with banana slices. Garnish with orange circles.

Makes approximately 20 2-inch pancakes or 12 4-inch pancakes.

* This recipe contains one-third egg per serving.
† May use any milk substitute—almond milk, soy milk, etc. See recipes in last chapter under variation recipes.
** Baking soda may be omitted in this recipe. However, pancakes will not be as light without it.

# PEACH SAUCE

**(Serves 6)**

4 cups fresh peaches,
   peeled and quartered
   (may use frozen or
   canned unsweetened)
Cinnamon to taste
   (optional)

1. Put peaches in blender with juice and blend until smooth. Flavor with cinnamon if desired.
2. Warm puree mixture in saucepan or in microwave just before serving.

Makes approximately 3 cups.

NUTRITIONAL ANALYSIS FOR MENU

Calories..................................................................................450
Fat .......................................................................................6.5g
Protein ...............................................................................16.6g
          U.S. RDA..................................................................36%
Cholesterol ........................................................................44mg
Sodium..............................................................................530mg
Carbohydrate......................................................................63.4g

# LUNCH

(LITE SUPPER):

- ◆**Sunny Day Luncheon**
- ◆**Picnic on the Patio**
- ◆**Mexican Fiesta**
- ◆**Baked Potato With the Works**
- ◆**Elegant Avenue Luncheon**
- ◆**Country-Time Lunch**
- ◆**Lunch in Italy**

NOTE: If following a therapeutic diet, please read Goals of This Book before continuing with the recipes.

# SUNNY DAY LUNCHEON

**Chilled California Fruit Soup**
**Homemade Wheat Thins**
**Peanut-Date Butter**
**Watermelon Star Salad**
**Iced Lemon-Mint Tea**

## CALIFORNIA FRUIT SOUP

(Serves 8)

1 cup water
1½ cups apricot nectar
3 tbsp. Minute Tapioca
2½ cups pineapple juice
¾ cup dried apricots, sliced thin
1 apple, diced
4 bananas, sliced
½ cup fresh strawberries, sliced (or any fresh berry)
½ cup frozen strawberries with juice
4 cups frozen or canned peaches with juice

1. Combine fruit juices, water, tapioca, and apricots in medium-sized saucepan.
2. Bring to boil; remove from heat and let stand 15 to 20 minutes.
3. Return to heat and bring to a boil; simmer approximately 5 to 10 minutes, stirring constantly, until tapioca granules are clear and soft.
4. Add sliced peaches, frozen strawberries, and diced apple. Simmer until hot. Add bananas and fresh strawberries. Serve hot, or cool in refrigerator and serve cold. Top with Cool Whip or whipped cream if desired.

# HOMEMADE WHEAT THINS

**(Serves 8-10)**

1½ cups whole-wheat pastry flour

½ tsp. salt (more or less to taste)

3 tbsp. brown sugar or 3 tbsp. molasses

2-4 tbsp. cold water

¼ cup vegetable oil

¼ cup peanut butter (optional)

1. Sift flour and salt; add brown sugar or molasses.
2. Pour water into oil, but do not mix.
3. Add peanut butter (optional) to flour mixture, mixing with a fork until crumbly. Lightly toss in water and oil until flour mixture is moistened. (May need more water if mixture is too dry.) Form dough into ball.
4. Place dough between wax paper and roll until thickness of piecrust. (The thinner dough is rolled, the crispier the cracker.)
5. Remove top wax paper and gently but quickly turn dough over onto cookie sheet. Remove remaining wax paper. Because thin edges burn easily, push them in to thicken edge.
6. Score top of dough into desired shapes (squares, triangles, strips, rectangles, circles, or cookie cutter designs).
7. Prick each cracker with a fork.
8. Bake at 375° F for 10 to 15 minutes until barely browned. Check often after 10 minutes. Outside edges may brown first and will need to be removed sooner.
9. Serve hot with fruit soup. Cool and dry thoroughly before storing in covered containers.

Makes 1 large cookie sheet.

# PEANUT-DATE BUTTER

**(Serves 24)**

½ cup hot water

½ cup pitted dates

½ cup peanut butter

1. Soak dates in hot water about 10 minutes.
2. Whiz water and dates in blender until smooth.
3. Add peanut butter; add more water if needed to thin.

Makes 1½ cups.

# WATERMELON STAR SALAD

½ slice medium water-
    melon (1 inch thick)
    Salad greens
½ cup low-fat cottage
    cheese
1 tbsp. blueberries

(Serves 1)

1. Cut watermelon into five wedges. Remove rind.
2. Arrange wedges on salad greens in a circle with points outward to resemble star.
3. Spoon cottage cheese into center of watermelon star. May use ice-cream scoop to make more attractive.
4. Sprinkle with blueberries. Serve.

# ICED LEMON-MINT TEA

1 cup boiling water
6 lemon-flavored decaf-
    feinated tea bags
2 tbsp. fresh mint leaves,
    crushed (may use 1 bag
    mint tea to replace)
6 oz. frozen lemonade
    concentrate, thawed
1 cup freshly squeezed
    orange juice (may
    use canned or frozen,
    reconstituted)
7½ cups cold water
    Fresh mint sprigs

(Serves 10-12)

1. Combine first three ingredients in a large container; cover and steep 5 minutes. Discard tea bags.
2. Stir in lemonade concentrate, orange juice, and cold water. Cover and chill overnight; strain before serving.
3. Pour over ice cubes in serving glasses; garnish with mint sprigs.

Makes 10 cups.

NUTRITIONAL ANALYSIS FOR MENU

Calories.................................................................................621
Fat....................................................................................17.7g
Protein..............................................................................22.2g
    U.S. RDA.....................................................................48%
Cholesterol.......................................................................10.3mg
Sodium............................................................................533mg
Carbohydrate....................................................................00.3g

# PICNIC ON THE PATIO

**Hot Corn Cartwheels**
**Hoagie Sandwiches**
**Quick Artichoke Pasta Salad**
**Lemonade Over Ice**

## HOT CORN CARTWHEELS

**4 ears of fresh corn**

(Serves 4)

1. Husk ears and remove silk just before cooking. Cut corn in 2-inch-wide slices to make cartwheels.
2. Place corn in enough unsalted cold water to cover. (Salt toughens corn.)
3. Add 1 tablespoon of sugar and 1 tablespoon of lemon juice to each gallon of water.
4. Heat to boiling; boil uncovered 2 minutes.
5. Remove from heat and serve. Add salt and margarine, if desired.

**To Microwave:** Wrap corn in waxed paper and twist ends. Microwave until tender, 7 to 9 minutes. Let stand 1 minute. Cut in 2-inch-wide slices and serve.

When shopping for corn, look for bright green husks, fresh-looking silk, plump but not too large kernels.

# HOAGIE SANDWICHES

1 hoagie bun
2 tsp. vegetable oil or
   Italian dressing
3 oz. sliced Mozzarella
   cheese*
3 tomato slices
   Lettuce leaves
   Salt
   Oregano

Optional vegetables:
   sweet onions, thinly
   sliced; cucumbers, sliced;
   green peppers, sliced;
   avocado, mashed and
   spread on bread, or sliced

*The authentic Italian hoagie would con-
tain provolone cheese. However, it is a
high-fat cheese. You may substitute a
mild cheddar, or delete cheese altogether.

(Serves 1)

1. Cut hoagie bun lengthwise, three-fourths of the way through.
2. Drizzle oil or dressing on opened bun. Squeeze sides together to soak in oil.
3. Place desired ingredients in bun, beginning with cheese.
4. May serve cold, or warm in oven or in microwave. Wrap in foil to warm in oven and add vegetables after bun and cheese have warmed. If desired, brown bun; do not wrap in foil, just lay bun on baking sheet and warm. If using microwave, follow same directions as oven except use Saran Wrap to cover. Be sure to cover in microwave and cook on medium high for no more than 1 minute to prevent bun from becoming tough.
5. Sprinkle with salt and oregano.

# QUICK ARTICHOKE PASTA SALAD

4 oz. salad macaroni

1 jar (6 oz.) marinated artichoke hearts

¼ lb. fresh small mush-rooms,

2 medium tomatoes, seeded and cut into bite-sized pieces

1 cup carrots, grated

1 cup medium pitted ripe olives

Salt to taste (optional)

(Serves 4-6)

1. Following package directions, cook macaroni in a large kettle of boiling water until tender.
2. Drain, rinse with cold water, and drain again. Turn into a large bowl.
3. Combine artichokes and their liquid, mushrooms, toma-toes, carrots, and olives. Add mixture to cooked pasta and toss gently. For additional moistness and seasoning, add Italian dressing.
4. Cover and refrigerate for at least 4 hours before serving. Season with salt to achieve desired taste (optional).

NUTRITIONAL ANALYSIS FOR MENU

Calories........................................................................592
Fat...........................................................................15.2g
Protein.....................................................................12.9g
     U.S. RDA...........................................................28%
Cholesterol..................................................................0mg
Sodium...................................................................693mg
Carbohydrate..............................................................103g

# MEXICAN FIESTA

Cheesy-Tomato Spanish Rice Soup
Ensalada Avocado
Flour Tortilla with Honey and Margarine
Piña Colada

## CHEESY-TOMATO SPANISH RICE SOUP

2 cups water

¾ cup long-grain brown rice, uncooked

2 cups (4 large stalks) finely chopped celery

1½ cups (2 medium) diced carrots

1-2 tsp. chili powder (optional)

8 cups tomato puree—4 lbs. chopped, unpeeled ripe tomatoes (or 3 1-lb. cans tomatoes and 2 cups water) blended until smooth

4 oz. (½ cup) canned mild green chilies, diced

1 tsp. ground cumin

(Serves 16)

1. In a 5- or 6-quart pot, bring water, rice, celery, carrots, and chili powder to a boil. Turn heat to low and simmer, covered tightly, for about a half hour, or until rice is slightly tender. (Check once or twice to make sure there is enough cooking water—add a little if necessary.)

2. Add pureed tomatoes and green chilies. Bring to a second boil. Cover, reduce heat and simmer, stirring occasionally, about 15 minutes, or until rice is tender.

3. Add cumin, garlic, and ripe chopped tomato, tomato paste, and water, and continue simmering about 10 minutes, or until flavors are well blended.

4. Turn burner to lowest heat. Add mozzarella cheese,

45

½ tsp. granulated garlic
1 large ripe tomato, chopped
1 6-oz. can tomato paste
1½ cups water
¼-½ lb. grated low-fat mozzarella
½ cup cottage cheese-sour cream (recipe, p. 110) or sour cream
¾ cup diced green onions sea salt to taste (optional)

sour cream and green onions, stirring quickly to blend well. Heat gently for 5 minutes (without boiling). Add salt to taste. Serve.

Leftovers keep well in refrigerated, sealed container. This also freezes well.
Makes 4 quarts.

*Variations:* May delete cheeses altogether and still have a wonderful low-fat Mexican soup.

# ENSALADA AVOCADO

Lettuce leaf
½ avocado, peeled
¼ cup cottage cheese
⅛ cup cucumber, peeled and diced
½ tsp. chives, chopped (fresh or dried)
½ tsp. pimento, chopped

(Serves 1)
1. Place lettuce leaf on individual salad plate.
2. Combine cottage cheese, cucumbers, and chives.
3. Scoop cottage cheese mixture into avocado and garnish with chopped pimento.

# PIÑA COLADA

(Serves 4-6)

1 cup pineapple juice,
    unsweetened
⅛ cup Coco Lopez—
    Cream of Coconut
½ cup club soda
2 cups ice
    Pineapple wedge
    Maraschino cherry to
    garnish

1. Mix pineapple juice, Coco Lopez, club soda, and ice in blender. Process until ice is slush. Stir between processing if needed. May add more club soda to obtain a thick, slushy consistency. May store in individual glasses in freezer for up to one hour (to prevent thoroughly freezing) if you want to make drinks ahead. Best if served immediately.
2. Garnish with pineapple wedge and maraschino cherry on a toothpick.

Makes 3½ to 4 cups.

NUTRITIONAL ANALYSIS FOR MENU

Calories ................................................................ 572
Fat ..................................................................... 27.2g
Protein ................................................................ 21g
    U.S. RDA ...................................................... 46%
Cholesterol .......................................................... 13mg
Sodium ............................................................... 1115mg
Carbohydrate ........................................................ 67g

# BAKED POTATO WITH THE WORKS

**Baked Potato Topped With Vegetables and Cheese Sauce**
**Spinach Salad**
**Whole-Wheat Mini Bread Loaves**
**Strawberry-Cider Cooler**

## BAKED POTATO TOPPED WITH VEGETABLES AND CHEESE SAUCE

(Serves 4)

**4 medium potatoes**

1. Scrub potatoes. Prick with fork to allow steam to escape. Wrap potatoes in tin foil and place on baking sheet.
2. Bake at 375° F for 1 to 1¼ hours; at 350° F for 1¼ to 1 ½ hours, or at 325° F for about 1½ hours, until soft.

**To Microwave:** Place potatoes in a covered casserole dish with approximately ½ cup of water. Cook on high for 10 minutes, turn potatoes and cook 5 minutes more, or until done. Drain water immediately to prevent potatoes from becoming soggy. Return lid to keep warm until serving.

3. To serve, cut crisscross gashes in tops; squeeze gently until some potato pops up through opening.
4. Top with cooked broccoli, cauliflower, and carrots. May use fresh or frozen vegetables and any vegetable combination of your choice.

(For tips on fresh-looking cooked vegetables that maintain their color, see directions following.)

5. Pour cheese sauce (recipe following) over vegetables and potato. Serve.

# BROCCOLI, CAULIFLOWER, AND CARROTS

2 cups broccoli, bite-sized flowerets

2 cups cauliflower, bite-sized flowerets

1 cup carrots, sliced (may use fresh or frozen vegetables)

(Serves 4-6)

1. In saucepan, bring ½ cup of water to a boil, then add vegetables. Cover.
2. After water returns to boil, remove lid for approximately 3 minutes to prevent discoloration of vegetables.
3. Replace lid until vegetables are barely tender, approximately 7 to 10 minutes. Drain and remove lid.

To Microwave: In covered casserole, place vegetables in ¼ cup of water. Cook on high for 5 minutes; stir and cook approximately 5 minutes longer. Let stand 1 minute; drain. Makes 5 cups.

# CHEESE SAUCE

½ stick of margarine

3½ tbsp. flour

2½ cups milk, skim*

¼ tsp. garlic powder, to taste

½ tsp. salt, to taste

1 cup mild cheddar cheese or low-fat mozzarella, chunked

2 tbsp. chives, fresh or dried

(Serves 4-6)

1. Heat margarine over low heat until melted.
2. Add flour, 1 tablespoon at a time, whisking with wire whip after each addition until smooth.
3. Add milk, 1 cup at a time, whisking with each addition until smooth.
4. Stir in cheese chunks until melted. Add chives and let simmer until sauce thickens. If too thick, add more milk. Serve over potatoes and vegetables.

To Microwave: Microwave margarine in 1½-quart glass dish for approximately 30 seconds on medium high or until melted. Stir in flour, garlic powder, and salt with fork. Gradually stir in milk. Microwave uncovered 1 minute; stir. Microwave 1 minute longer or until smooth and thick; stir. Add cheese and chives and microwave uncovered until cheese is melted and sauce has thickened, approximately 1 to 1½ minutes. May need to add more milk. Makes approximately 4 cups.

*May use any milk substitute—almond milk, soy milk, etc. See recipes in last chapter under variation recipes.

# SPINACH SALAD

2 tbsp. lemon juice
¾ tsp. salt or seasoning
1 small clove garlic,
  crushed
8 oz. fresh mushrooms,
  sliced (about 3 cups)
16 oz. spinach, torn into
  bite-sized pieces
¼ cup vegetable oil

(Serves 4-6)

1. Mix lemon juice, salt, garlic; toss with mushrooms and let stand 15 minutes.
2. Toss spinach and oil until leaves glisten.
3. Toss mushroom mixture with spinach. Garnish with sunflower seeds and tomato wedges.

# WHOLE-WHEAT MINI BREAD LOAVES

*Directions for using food processor or bread maker:*

2 tbsp. sugar (may replace
  with honey)
3 tsp. salt
2 pkgs. active dry yeast
  (may use fast-rising)
3 cups whole wheat flour
3-3½ cups all-purpose flour
2 cups warm water (120-
  130° F)
⅓ cup margarine
⅓ cup molasses and honey
  combined

1. In food processor combine sugar, salt, yeast, 2 cups whole-wheat flour, and 1 cup all-purpose flour.
2. In separate bowl combine warm water, margarine chunks, and molasses/honey. Mix together. Margarine does not need to completely melt.
3. Add liquid mixture to dry ingredients. Process approximately 30 seconds. Scrape bowl with rubber spatula and process another 10 seconds until completely mixed.
4. Add ½ cup whole-wheat flour and ½ cup all-purpose flour. Process until additional flour is moistened.
5. Add additional ½ cup whole-wheat flour and process until flour is moistened. Add remaining 1½ cups all-purpose flour, processing after each ½ cup addition until flour is moistened.
6. Dough should be slightly sticky to touch, but firm. If dough is too sticky, add an additional ½ to ¾ cup flour, making sure that flour is completely mixed into dough.
7. Oil your hands and working surface. Remove dough from processor, place on working surface. Shape dough into ball and place in greased, large bowl, turning dough to grease top. Cover with towel; let rise in warm, draft-free place, 80° to 85° F, until doubled, about 1 hour.

8a.  *If using the fast-rising yeast:* Shape dough into loaves and place directly into greased bread pans. May use mini-loaf pans or two regular loaf pans. Lightly grease tops of loaves, cover with towel; let rise in warm, draft-free place, 80° to 85° F until doubled. Place self-rising loaves directly into pre-heated oven. Bake mini loaves in 400° F oven approximately 20 minutes or until golden brown, and loaves sound hollow when lightly tapped with fingers. Bake regular loaves approximately 30 minutes. Immediately remove from pans to cooling rack. Brush tops of loaves with oil to soften crusts, if desired.

8b.  *If using regular yeast:* Punch down raised dough; turn onto lightly floured surface; cut in half, cover with bowl; let dough rest for 15 minutes for easier shaping. Grease bread pans. With lightly floured rolling pin, roll each dough half into a rectangle, approximately 1 inch thick. Starting at narrow end, roll dough up tightly and pinch the edge with fingers. Seal ends by pressing them with the sides of your hands and fold them under. Place the roll, seam side down, in loaf pan. Repeat with second half of dough. If using mini loaves, use same procedure for amount of dough needed to fill pans to ½ full. Cover loaves with towel; let rise in warm place, away from draft, until loaves are doubled, about 1 hour. Preheat oven to 400° F, bake regular loaves approximately 30 minutes; mini loaves approximately 20 minutes, until golden brown and when loaves sound hollow when lightly tapped with fingers. Remove to cooling racks. Brush oil on tops of loaves to soften crusts, if desired.

# STRAWBERRY-CIDER COOLER

2 cups fresh strawberries, washed and hulled

2 cups sparkling cider, chilled (May use 1 cup apple cider and 1 cup club soda to make sparkling cider)

1 cup club soda, chilled

(Serves 6)

1. Place strawberries in blender; process until smooth.
2. Press strawberries through a sieve lined with two layers of cheesecloth; lift cheesecloth from sieve and squeeze to drain remaining juice. Discard seeds.
3. Transfer juice to a large pitcher; stir in cider and soda.

Makes 4 cups

NUTRITIONAL ANALYSIS FOR MENU

Calories.................................................................................................586
Fat ....................................................................................................17.6g
Protein...............................................................................................25.3g
    U.S. RDA .....................................................................................55%
Cholesterol......................................................................................17.5mg
Sodium ...........................................................................................776mg
Carbohydrate.....................................................................................87.8g

# ELEGANT AVENUE LUNCHEON

**Fettuccine Verde**
**Buttered Spring Vegetables**
**Fruit Juice Refresher**

## FETTUCCINE VERDE

(Serves 4)

1 8-oz. package medium-wide fettuccine noodles

3 tbsp. margarine

1 cup green onion with tops, sliced

2 cloves garlic, minced or pressed

1 cup low-fat milk* or may use half and half for richer taste

1 cup mozzarella cheese, grated

⅛ tsp. ground nutmeg
Salt to taste
Parmesan cheese (optional)
Cherry tomato or carrot curls to garnish

1. Cook noodles in a large kettle of boiling water, following package directions.
2. Drain.
3. While noodles are cooking, melt margarine in a wide frying pan over medium-high heat. Add green onions and garlic and cook, stirring for 2 minutes.
4. Add milk and heat until bubbling.
5. Add hot noodles to pan and toss gently.
6. Add ½ cup of the cheese and toss until noodles are evenly coated. Add remaining cheese. Toss again.
7. Season with nutmeg and salt to taste, then toss again.
8. If desired, sprinkle with Parmesan cheese, or fresh grated Parmesan for individual servings. Garnish with cherry tomatoes.

NOTE: This dish takes approximately 10 to 15 minutes to prepare. Best if served immediately to prevent sticky noodles.

*May use any milk substitute—almond milk, soy milk, etc.
See recipes in last chapter under variation recipes.

# BUTTERED SPRING VEGETABLES

½ lb. slender, fresh green
    beans, trimmed
½ lb. baby carrots or French
    carrots, trimmed, pared
½ small cabbage
2 tbsp. unsalted margarine
2 tbsp. minced fresh parsley
    Salt (optional)

(Serves 4)

1. Cook beans in large saucepan of boiling water until crisp-tender, about 7 minutes. Remove beans with slotted spoon. Rinse under cold running water until cold; drain thoroughly.
2. Add carrots to boiling water; cook until crisp-tender, about 9 minutes. Rinse under cold running water until cool; drain thoroughly.
3. For cabbage, remove outside leaves; wash. Leave core in place to hold wedge together until cooked. Add cabbage to ½ inch of boiling water. Cover and steam until crisp-tender, 8 to 10 minutes. Drain.

**To Microwave:** Place carrots and ¼ cup water in small casserole dish. Microwave covered on high until carrots are partially tender, 5 minutes. Stir and cook approximately 3 minutes longer until done. Drain.

Place beans in ¼ cup water in small casserole dish. Microwave, covered on high until crisp-tender, about 6 minutes. Stir and cook approximately 2 to 3 minutes longer until done. Drain.

Place cabbage in 2 tablespoons water in small casserole dish.

Microwave covered on high until crisp-tender, about 7 minutes. Drain.

Microwave margarine, uncovered, in glass serving bowl on high power until melted, about 1½ to 2 minutes. Stir in vegetables; microwave, uncovered, until vegetables are heated through, about 2 minutes. Sprinkle with parsley and salt to taste; cool to tepid.

4. Melt margarine in medium-sized skillet over medium-low heat; add vegetables. Cook, shaking pan occasionally, until vegetables are heated through, about 4 minutes. Sprinkle with parsley; add salt to taste if desired.
5. Serve, placing vegetables separately on plate.

# FRUIT JUICE REFRESHER

**(Serves 8-10)**

24 oz. club soda, chilled
24 oz. peach nectar, chilled
1 cup unsweetened orange juice, chilled
½ cup unsweetened grapefruit juice, chilled
¼ cup lemon juice, chilled
Orange rind strips

1. Combine first five ingredients in a large pitcher; mix well.
2. Pour over ice cubes in serving glasses.
3. Garnish with strips of orange rind.

Makes 2 quarts.

NUTRITIONAL ANALYSIS FOR MENU

Calories..................................................................................................532
Fat .......................................................................................................19g
Protein ................................................................................................17.7g
    U.S. RDA ......................................................................................38%
Cholesterol........................................................................................17.5mg
Sodium..............................................................................................342mg
Carbohydrate.......................................................................................76.5g

# COUNTRY-TIME LUNCH

Dutch Potato Soup
Broiled Asparagus and Cheese Open-faced Sandwich
Apple Juice

## DUTCH POTATO SOUP

1 medium onion, chopped
6 medium potatoes, sliced
3-4 cups water, to cover
1 cup evaporated skim milk*
1 cup small-curd cottage cheese, low-fat
1 tbsp. parsley flakes

(Serves 6)

1. Place potatoes, onions, and water in soup kettle. Simmer until tender.
2. Add evaporated milk, bring just to a boil and gently stir in cottage cheese and parsley flakes. May sprinkle individual servings with grated cheese.

*May use any milk substitute—almond milk, soy milk, etc.
See recipes in last chapter under variation recipes.

## ASPARAGUS AND CHEESE OPEN-FACED SANDWICH

1 slice whole-grain bread
1 tsp. margarine (optional)
6-8 asparagus spears, fresh-cooked or canned
2 tsp. onion, chopped (optional)
2 oz. mozzarella cheese, thinly sliced
Tomato slices

(Serves 1)

1. Spread margarine on bread.
2. Lay asparagus spears lengthwise on bread. Sprinkle with chopped onion and top with cheese slices.
3. Place sandwich in preheated 450° F oven for 8 to 10 minutes or until cheese is melted. May broil 1 minute for additional browning and crispness.
4. Serve immediately. Garnish with tomato slices.

NUTRITIONAL ANALYSIS FOR MENU

| | |
|---|---|
| Calories | 502 |
| Fat | 11.6g |
| Protein | 332g |
| U.S. RDA | 69% |
| Cholesterol | 52.1mg |
| Sodium | 664mg |
| Carbohydrate | 68.7g |

# LUNCH IN ITALY

**Eggplant Parmesan**
**Italian Vegetable Toss**
**Italian Oven Bread**
**Chilled Grape Juice**

# EGGPLANT PARMESAN

(Serves 5)

1 medium eggplant
1 egg*
¾ cup bread crumbs
2-4 tbsp. oil

1. Wash eggplant (peeling is optional).
2. Slice ½ inch thick.
3. Beat egg in bowl large enough to dip eggplant into. Add 1 to 2 tablespoons of water or milk to stretch egg mixture.
4. Put bread crumbs in bowl large enough to dip eggplant in. May use whole-wheat flour seasoned with garlic powder, parsley, basil, and oregano to replace bread crumbs.
5. Heat nonstick skillet, using a very small amount of oil if desired. Brown eggplant on both sides. May put in oven and bake on cookie sheet until tender or put under broiler to brown just a few minutes.
6. Layer cooked eggplant in flat casserole dish, covering each layer with tomato sauce. (Use recipe following or purchase canned sauce.)
7. May sprinkle with mozzarella cheese or Parmesan cheese if desired.
8. Put casserole in oven and cook at approximately 350° F until sauce is bubbly. Serve immediately.

\* This recipe contains one-fifth egg per serving.

# TOMATO SAUCE

1 qt. canned tomatoes
9 oz. tomato paste
½ green pepper, quartered or chopped
1 tsp. oregano
1 tsp. sweet basil
3 garlic cloves, minced or pressed
1 tsp. onion salt (may use fresh onion if desired)
1 bay leaf
Dash of sugar
Dash of lemon juice

(Makes 5-6 cups)

1. In large pan, simmer all ingredients. The longer it simmers, the more flavor the sauce will have. Cook a half hour minimum or until vegetables are done.
2. Remove quartered green pepper and bay leaf before serving.
3. May add mushrooms, onions, etc., to sauce while simmering.

# ITALIAN VEGETABLE TOSS

1 ½ cups shell macaroni
2 cups broccoli flowerets
1 cup cauliflower flowerets
1 cup sliced fresh mushrooms
1 6-oz. can artichoke hearts, drained and chopped (may use marinated)
1 cup pitted black olives
½ cup green onion, chopped
1 medium avocado, sliced
1 medium tomato, chopped
⅔ cup Italian salad dressing (may use prepared dressing)

(Serves 12)

1. Cook 1½ cups macaroni according to package directions. Drain and rinse with cold water; drain well.
2. Combine macaroni, broccoli, cauliflower, mushrooms, artichoke hearts, black olives, and green onions.
3. Toss with Italian dressing. Cover and chill several hours.
4. To serve, toss vegetable mixture with avocado and tomato, leaving a few slices of each out to garnish.

# ITALIAN DRESSING

⅓-½ cup vegetable oil
2 tbsp. lemon juice
1 garlic clove, pressed
1 tbsp. fresh parsley, chopped
½ tsp salt

(Makes ⅔ cup)

1. Mix all ingredients together, shake, and refrigerate. Shake again before serving.

NUTRITIONAL ANALYSIS FOR MENU

| | |
|---|---|
| Calories | 528 |
| Fat | 19g |
| Protein | 13.3g |
| U.S. RDA | 29% |
| Cholesterol | 52.6mg |
| Sodium | 759mg |
| Carbohydrate | 80.2g |

# DINNER

- **A Light and Refreshing Vegetable Dinner**
- **Dinner With an Oriental Flair**
- **Dinner Fit for a Caesar**
- **Enjoy an Evening in Greece**
- **The All-American Family Dinner**
- **It's Italian Night**
- **West Coast Garden Dinner**

NOTE: If following a therapeutic diet, please read Goals of This Book before continuing with the recipes.

# A LIGHT AND REFRESHING VEGETABLE DINNER

New Red Potatoes and Vegetables
with Sour Cream and Cheese
Garden Fresh Tossed Salad with Herb Dressing
Crusty Hard Rolls
Banana Fruit Punch
Strawberry Romanoff

10 small red potatoes
1 pint sour cream*
½ cup green onions, thinly sliced
½ cup fresh tomatoes, cored and chopped
1 cup bite-sized cauliflower flowerets
1 cup carrots, thinly sliced
1 cup bite-sized broccoli flowerets (may use fresh or frozen vegetables)
1½ cups finely shredded cheddar cheese (may use Monterey Jack or mozzarella to lower fat content or delete)

## NEW RED POTATOES AND VEGETABLES WITH SOUR CREAM AND CHEESE

(Serves 4)

1. Scrub potatoes and boil in small amount of water until tender. If you use too much water, the skins will loosen.

**To Microwave:** Put a small amount of water in covered casserole dish and steam approximately 15 minutes on high until tender.

2. Split potatoes in half and arrange in 8" x 8" (approximate size) serving dish with cut sides up.

3. Combine sour cream, green onions, and tomatoes. Stir well and pour over hot potatoes.

*May use any milk substitute—almond milk, soy milk, etc.
See recipes in last chapter under variation recipes.

4. Lightly steam cauliflower, carrots, and broccoli in small amount of water until barely tender. Drain and arrange on top of dressed potatoes.

**To Microwave:** Put vegetables in covered casserole dish in small amount of water and cook on high for approximately 10 minutes (until barely tender). Drain and arrange on top of dressed potatoes.

5. Sprinkle cheese over all (optional). Best when served immediately to keep vegetables and potatoes hot while sour cream and tomatoes stay cool.

*See variations for sour cream in last chapter.

# GARDEN FRESH TOSSED SALAD WITH HERB DRESSING

**(Serves 6)**

1. Rinse and dry all vegetables.
2. In large bowl, tear lettuce into bite-sized pieces. Take out center stems of spinach leaves and discard. Tear spinach leaves into bite-sized pieces, mixing with lettuce. Add carrots, cucumbers, and onion rings and toss. Cover and chill until serving time.
3. Add herb salad dressing (recipe following) or use dressing of choice and toss. Garnish with cherry tomatoes and serve immediately.

8 cups fresh green leaf lettuce
2 cups fresh spinach leaves
½ cup carrots, shredded
½ cup cucumbers, peeled and sliced
½ cup red onions, cut in thin slices separated in rings
Red, ripe cherry tomatoes

NUTRITIONAL ANALYSIS FOR MENU

| | |
|---|---|
| Calories | 686 |
| Fat | 14.9g |
| Protein | 23.9g |
| U.S. RDA | 52% |
| Cholesterol | 13.5mg |
| Sodium | 780mg |
| Carbohydrate | 129g |

⅓ cup water
⅓ cup vegetable oil
⅛ cup lemon juice
1 small garlic clove, crushed (or use ¼ tsp. garlic powder)
⅛ tsp. sweet basil
⅛ tsp. oregano
⅛ tsp. parsley (dried)
¼ tsp. honey
Salt to taste (optional)

# HERB SALAD DRESSING

(Serves 10-12)

Mix all ingredients. Chill until ready to use. Shake before each use.

---

6-oz. can frozen orange juice concentrate
6-oz. can frozen lemonade concentrate
½ cup unsweetened pineapple juice
3 small bananas, chunked

# BANANA FRUIT PUNCH

(Serves 8-10)

1. Dilute frozen concentrated juices as directed on cans. Chill thoroughly or use ice water.
2. Whiz bananas and juices in blender just before serving. Makes 6 to 7 cups.

---

1 pint fresh, unhulled strawberries
⅛ cup sour cream*
⅛ cup Cool Whip
¼ cup brown sugar (optional)

# STRAWBERRY ROMANOFF

(Serves 4)

1. Wash strawberries leaving stems on.
2. Mix sour cream (or substitute) and Cool Whip.
3. Serve strawberries, sour cream mixture, and brown sugar in separate bowls. Place small amount of each on individual plates, and dip strawberries into sour cream mixture and then into brown sugar and eat. A simple yet delicious way to end a meal.

*See variations for sour cream in last chapter.

# DINNER WITH AN ORIENTAL FLAIR

**Vegetable Tofu Stir-Fry**
**Whole-Grain Rice**
**Oriental Asparagus With Sesame Seed Sauce**
**Crimson Banana Delight**
**Garnish of Fortune Cookie**
**Hot Herbal Tea**

## VEGETABLES AND TOFU STIR-FRY

1 block firm tofu, cubed
1 medium onion, sliced or chopped or 5 green onions, sliced using tops
2 tbsp. margarine
3 tbsp. soy sauce, lite
2 garlic cloves, pressed or minced
3 large carrots, thinly sliced
1½ cups broccoli, bite-sized pieces
1½ cups cauliflower, bite-sized pieces (may use 22 oz. of frozen broccoli, cauliflower, and carrot mix). May add tomatoes, mushrooms, celery, cabbage, bean sprouts, etc., in the amount of your preference

(Serves 4-6)

1. Sauté tofu cubes, onion, garlic cloves, and margarine until browned. Add soy sauce to taste. Remove from pan.
2. In same skillet* with remaining margarine, add carrots, broccoli, cauliflower, and any other variety of vegetables of choice. Cover and steam until vegetables are barely tender, approximately 8 to 10 minutes.
3. Add tofu mixture to cooked vegetables and carefully stir together so tofu does not fall apart.
4. May add fresh tomatoes to mixture, just barely warming before serving to maintain crispness. Serve.

*May use wok, but reduce the cooking time.

# WHOLE-GRAIN RICE

(Serves 6)

1 cup brown rice, un-
cooked
2 cups water
1 tsp. salt

1. Heat rice, water, and salt to boiling, stirring once or twice; reduce heat.
2. Cover and simmer 30 to 40 minutes. (Do not lift cover or stir.)
3. Remove from heat. Fluff rice lightly with fork; cover and let steam 5 to 10 minutes longer.
4. Serve on the side or use as a bed for the Vegetable Tofu Stir-Fry.

# ORIENTAL ASPARAGUS WITH SESAME SEED SAUCE

(Serves 4)

1-2 lb. fresh asparagus
(may use frozen if fresh
is not available)
Sesame Seed Sauce:
1-1½ tsp. sesame seeds,
toasted*
2 tbsp. soy sauce, lite
1 tbsp. sugar

1. Boil asparagus in salted water for a few minutes, or until tender.
2. Immediately drain and rinse with cold water and ice cubes to stop the cooking process. Completely drain again and pat dry with paper towels. Place asparagus in medium-sized bowl.
3. Place soy sauce in small mixing bowl and add the sugar, stirring completely to dissolve.
4. Pour this sauce over asparagus and mix gently.
5. Cover and refrigerate, occasionally spooning sauce over asparagus.
6. Sprinkle toasted sesame seeds over asparagus and serve at room temperature.

May use for a before-dinner appetizer also.

*To toast sesame seeds, place them in a heavy skillet *without* oil and cook over high heat, shaking constantly, for 1 to 2 minutes.

# CRIMSON BANANA DELIGHT

**(Serves 4)**

2 packages (10 oz. each) frozen sweetened raspberries

4 ripe bananas

3 tsp. fresh lemon juice

2 tbsp. sliced unblanched almonds

4 fortune cookies (optional)

1. Place *unopened* raspberry packages in large bowl; add hot tap water to cover. Set aside to thaw.
2. Drain thawed raspberries, reserving ¼ cup of the syrup. (Reserve remaining syrup for another use.)
3. Peel bananas; cut diagonally into ¼-inch slices. Arrange on four individual dessert plates in sunburst pattern; brush or drizzle with 2 teaspoons of the lemon juice.
4. Mound raspberries in center of bananas, dividing evenly. Mix ¼ cup reserved syrup and remaining 1 teaspoon of lemon juice. Spoon over raspberries, dividing evenly. Refrigerate, covered.
5. At serving time, sprinkle desserts with almonds; garnish with fortune cookie if desired.

NUTRITIONAL ANALYSIS FOR MENU

| | |
|---|---|
| Calories | 506 |
| Fat | 7.8g |
| Protein | 18.5g |
| U.S. RDA | 33% |
| Cholesterol | 0mg |
| Sodium | 1165mg |
| Carbohydrate | 96.6g |

# DINNER FIT FOR A CAESAR

**Vegetable Lasagna**
**Stuffed and Broiled Tomatoes**
**Melon-Cucumber Salad**
**Garlic Bread**
**Peach-Banana Sherbet**
**Grape Juice Crush**

## VEGETABLE LASAGNA

8 oz. lasagna noodles
1 small onion, chopped
½ pound mushrooms, sliced
3 small zucchini squash, thinly sliced
4 carrots, sliced
1 cup spinach, chopped
6 oz. Jack cheese, shredded
2 cups cottage cheese
¼ cup green onions or chives, finely sliced
2 eggs (optional)*
⅓ cup Parmesan cheese (optional)
½ tsp. salt
1 garlic clove, crushed or minced
⅛ tsp. oregano
⅛ tsp. basil
⅛ tsp. thyme

(Serves 6)

1. Boil and drain noodles.
2. Steam onion, mushrooms, zucchini, and carrots in small amount of water until tender.
3. Add 1 cup chopped spinach and continue cooking until spinach is warmed. Add spices.
4. In separate bowl, mix cottage cheese, green onion and eggs.
5. In 13" x 9" x 2" pan, layer noodles, vegetable mixture, cottage cheese mixture (spooned on top of vegetables into two 2" strips), grated Jack cheese and then Parmesan cheese if using Parmesan.
6. Repeat step 5, ending with cheeses to obtain a crispy, brown top layer.
7. Bake uncovered at 375° F for 40 to 50 minutes or until top is slightly browned.

* If using eggs, this recipe contains one-third egg per serving.

# STUFFED AND BROILED TOMATOES

(Serves 6-8)

6-8 medium-sized tomatoes
½ large zucchini, fresh, cubed
1 small onion (may use green onion)
6-8 fresh mushrooms, sliced thinly (optional)
1½- 2 cups cooked rice (3/4 cup uncooked)
½ tsp. basil
½ tsp. oregano
½ tsp. garlic salt

1. Steam first four ingredients in small amount of water until vegetables are soft. Add seasonings and rice. If adding uncooked rice, allow appropriate cooking time. (Example: Minute Rice needs to sit for only 5 minutes and it is done. Great if you don't have much time! Brown rice should be precooked and added to vegetables.)
2. Rinse, core, and remove tomato seeds, cutting a neat opening in top of tomato to accommodate a teaspoon.
3. Stuff tomatoes with filling.
4. Sprinkle with Parmesan cheese or another grated cheese if desired.
5. Bake in 350° F oven for 15 minutes or until tomato is slightly soft and cheese is melted.

# MELON-CUCUMBER SALAD

(Serves 4)

1 medium cucumber
2 cups cantaloupe, honey-dew, and/or watermelon
Salad greens

1. Thinly slice cucumber.
2. Cut melons into ¾-inch chunks.
3. Toss together and serve over salad greens on individual plates.

## NUTRITIONAL ANALYSIS FOR MENU

Calories.................................................................................658
Fat .....................................................................................13.7g
Protein ...............................................................................33.7g
    U.S. RDA ....................................................................73%
Cholesterol.........................................................................33.1mg
Sodium...............................................................................945mg
Carbohydrate.....................................................................110g

# PEACH AND BANANA SHERBET

1 cup skim milk*
1-2 medium-sized ripe peaches, peeled and cut in ½-inch chunks to make 1 cup
Sugar to taste
½ banana

(Serves 6)

1. Pour milk into an ice cube tray; freeze.
2. Chill fruit well or freeze.
3. Shortly before serving, remove milk and peaches, if frozen, from freezer.
4. Let stand about 5 minutes at room temperature.
5. Remove milk cubes from tray; cut them into small chunks if cubes are large.
6. In food processor, whirl one third of the frozen milk pieces at a time, using on-off bursts to break up the ice. Process continuously until velvety smooth.
7. Drop in peaches (one third at a time) banana chunks and sugar; process until smooth.

*Variations:* If you don't have a food processor, place all the ice in a mixing bowl and smash it into small pieces with a wooden spoon. Then beat with electric beater until smooth—slowly at first, gradually increasing to higher speeds. Puree peaches in a blender, adding 2 to 4 tablespoons milk to start blender if needed. Beat fruit puree into milk slush. Stir in sugar to taste.

8. For a soft sherbet, serve immediately.
9. If texture is too soft, store mixture in freezer until it reaches desired firmness, or serve a slushy shake.
10. Freeze leftover sherbet; let it soften at room temperature 15 to 20 minutes before serving.

Makes approximately 3 cups.

*May use any milk substitute—almond milk, soy milk, etc. See recipes in last chapter under variation recipes.

# GRAPE JUICE CRUSH

24 oz. grape juice, chilled
1 cup orange juice, chilled
⅛ cup lemon juice, chilled
⅛ cup sugar (optional)
32 oz. club soda

(Serves 10)

1. Mix juices and sugar until sugar is dissolved.
2. Just before serving, stir in soda. Serve over ice.

Makes 8 cups.

# ENJOY AN EVENING IN GREECE

**Tzatziki With Hard Bread**
(Cucumber and Yogurt Dip)

**Spanakopita**
(Spinach Pie)

**Domatasalata**
(Greek Salad)

**Fresh Cantaloupe and Kiwi Compote**

**Iced Lemon Water**

## TZATZIKI

(Cucumber and Yogurt Dip)

(Serves 4-6)

1 tbsp. olive oil
1 tsp. lemon juice
1 garlic clove, crushed
6 oz. plain low-fat yogurt
¼ cucumber, peeled, seeded, and grated fine
Salt to taste
Black olives to garnish

1. Mix olive oil and lemon juice.
2. Add garlic, yogurt, cucumber, and salt.
3. Garnish with black olives.

A wonderful appetizer served with hard bread, cucumbers, and eggplant.

Makes approximately 1 cup.

# SPANAKOPITA

(Spinach Pie)

(Serves 6)

2 lb. fresh spinach (may use frozen chopped)

1 large onion, sliced finely or diced

1 bunch spring green onions, sliced

4 tbsp. melted margarine for pastry

Salt to taste

4-5 tbsp. finely chopped parsley

3-4 tbsp. chopped dill

8 oz. white feta cheese, crumbled or grated low-fat mozzarella cheese

3-4 eggs, separated*

1 lb. Fyllo pastry (purchased in refrigerated section of supermarket)

1. In covered skillet steam onions in a small amount of water.
2. Shred spinach coarsely and add, stirring over medium heat.
3. Cover and cook 5 to 6 minutes. Add salt, parsley, and dill, cooking slightly.
4. Beat egg whites slightly, add two yolks (remaining yolks not used) and crumble feta cheese into eggs, then add to drained spinach mixture.
5. Place seven to eight layers of Fyllo pastry in bottom of 8" x 8" square dish—brushing margarine on each layer to add crispness. Pour mixture over pastry layers.
6. Add six to seven more layers of Fyllo pastry on top, buttering each layer again.
7. Cut diamond or triangle shapes in top pastry only, before baking. (Pastry is too crumbly to cut after it is cooked.)
8. Bake at 375° F for 40 minutes or until golden brown and crisp. Let stand 5 minutes and cut in marked places into bottom layers. Serve.

* This recipe contains one-half egg per serving.

3 medium tomatoes, cut into thin wedges

1 onion, sliced in thin rings

1 green pepper, sliced

3-4 tbsp. olive oil

2 tbsp. lemon juice

1 cucumber, peeled and cut in small chunks

Feta cheese, approximately 1 cup, or to taste

Salt to taste

1 pinch oregano

Black olives to garnish

# DOMATASALATA

(Greek Salad)

(Serves 6-8)

1. Mix all ingredients except black olives and let marinate overnight.
2. Garnish with olives and serve.

Makes 4 cups.

# FRESH CANTALOUPE AND KIWI COMPOTE

1. In a clear sherbet dish, place peeled, chunked cantaloupe.
2. Garnish with three slices of kiwi resting on edge of the dish.

A wonderfully simple dessert that is healthful and attractive. The Greek desserts are usually fresh fruit, simply prepared.

# ICED LEMON WATER

Squeeze lemon wedge or circle into ice water and garnish with lemon on edge of glass.

NUTRITIONAL ANALYSIS FOR MENU

| | |
|---|---|
| Calories | 449 |
| Fat | 21.4g |
| Protein | 25g |
| U.S. RDA | 54% |
| Cholesterol | 120mg |
| Sodium | 371mg |
| Carbohydrate | 47.8g |

# THE ALL-AMERICAN FAMILY DINNER

**Special K Meatloaf**
**Twice-baked Potato**
**Layered Salad**
**Cloverleaf Dinner Rolls**
**Peach Cobbler**
**Foamy Lemon Refresher**

## SPECIAL K MEATLOAF

(Serves 12-15)

2 pints cottage cheese
  (small curd best)
5 packages George Wash-
  ington Broth or MBT
  vegetable broth
1 stick melted margarine
5 eggs, large*
1 cup walnuts, chopped
1 large onion, chopped
12 oz. box of Special K
  cereal

1. Mix all ingredients together in a very large bowl, adding cereal last, and spread in 13″ x 9″ x 2″ baking pan lightly sprayed with Pam. Mixture will be quite thick.
2. Bake at 350° F for one hour. May freeze before baking for later use.

*Variations:* Tofu Special K Meatloaf
Replace cottage cheese and eggs with two 16-oz. packages of tofu (soft—mashed, or regular—blended till smooth in blender or food processor). When using tofu, add one extra package of vegetable broth. Bake at 350° F for one hour or until browned and crispy. (May take longer.) There is very little difference in flavor when using tofu—surprisingly! The main difference is the texture may be softer compared to the regular recipe's crispiness.

\* This recipe contains one-third egg per serving.

NUTRITIONAL ANALYSIS FOR MENU

| | |
|---|---|
| Calories | 716 |
| Fat | 24.9g |
| Protein | 23.8g |
| U.S. RDA | 52% |
| Cholesterol | 94mg |
| Sodium | 833mg |
| Carbohydrate | 112g |

# TWICE-BAKED POTATOES

**(Serves 4-6)**

6 large baking potatoes
  Margarine to taste
  Salt to taste
  Milk,* if needed
  Garnishes: green onions,
    paprika, or cheese

1. Scrub baking potatoes and bake at 350 to 400° F until done.
2. Slice potato lengthwise and scoop out insides of potato, being careful to preserve the skins for refilling.
3. Mash scooped-out portion with potato masher or hand mixer, adding margarine and salt to taste while mixing. If too dry to mix, add a small amount of milk or soy milk. Milk will give you a creamier texture.
4. Put mashed potatoes back into skins. Sprinkle with green onions, paprika, or cheese, etc.
5. Put in 425° F oven until mashed portion is browned. Serve.

*May use any milk substitute—almond milk, soy milk, etc. See recipes in last chapter under variation recipes.

# LAYERED SALAD

**(Serves 8-10)**

1 head dark green leafy
    lettuce of choice
2 cups purple cabbage,
    shredded
2 cups carrots, shredded
2 cups frozen peas
  Mayonnaise, low-fat or
    ranch dressing
  Sugar

  Garnishes:
    Tomato wedges or
      cherry tomatoes
    Avocado wedges
    Baco Bits

1. Fill large, clear glass bowl three-quarters full with torn lettuce, slightly pressed down. (Tearing prevents browning of lettuce.)
2. Layer cabbage, carrots, and peas in this order.
3. Top with ½ inch layer of mayonnaise. Sprinkle lightly with sugar. May use ranch dressing instead of mayonnaise and sugar.
4. Refrigerate overnight to blend flavors. (This is important if using mayonnaise and sugar topping.)
5. Garnish just before serving.

*Variations for mayonnaise:* Yogurt-Herb Dressing (recipe following) is a great replacement for mayonnaise and also great for any salad dressing or sandwich spread. Delete sugar if using Yogurt-Herb Dressing on Layered Salad.

# YOGURT-HERB DRESSING

(Serves 30-35)

2 cups plain low-fat Yogurt
⅓ cup lemon juice
1 tsp. onion salt
½ tsp. garlic salt

1. Combine all ingredients and mix. Let stand 15 minutes to marinate flavors.
2. Cover and refrigerate until served.

Makes 2⅓ cups.

# PEACH COBBLER

(Serves 8-10)

4 cups ripe peaches, peeled and sliced
3 tbsp. sugar (may replace with honey)
1 tbsp. quick-cooking tapioca, uncooked
1 tbsp. lemon juice
½ tsp. ground cinnamon
⅛ tsp. ground cloves
1 cup all-purpose flour
1 tbsp. sugar
3 tbsp. cold margarine, cut into bits
4-5 tbsp. skim milk*

1. Combine first 6 ingredients in a 9-inch pie plate; toss well. Let stand 20 to 30 minutes.
2. Combine flour and sugar in a medium bowl; cut in margarine with a pastry cutter until mixture resembles coarse meal. Stir in milk with a fork to form dough into a ball.
3. Roll dough into a 10-inch circle on a lightly floured surface; place over filling in pie plate. Trim edges evenly around pie plate, leaving ½- to 1-inch overlap. Fold edges under, making pastry edge even with pie plate edge. Flute edge decoratively; chill 30 minutes. Cut slits in top to allow steam to escape. May sprinkle with 2 teaspoons fine sugar if desired.
4. Bake at 375° F for 30 minutes or until crust is golden and filling is bubbly.

* May use any milk substitute—almond milk, soy milk, etc. See recipe in last chapter under variation recipes.

# FOAMY LEMON REFRESHER

(Serves 8)

12 oz. lemonade concentrate, frozen
2¼ cups water
2¼ cups sugar-free 7-Up or ginger ale, chilled

1. Mix frozen lemonade concentrate with water; pour into ice cube trays. Freeze until slushy.
2. Mix chilled carbonated beverage with lemonade slush just before serving. Garnish with fresh fruit—lemon wedge, strawberry, cherry, etc.

Makes 6 cups.

# IT'S ITALIAN NIGHT

**Pasta With Tomato Sauce**
**Pecan Meatballs**
**Tossed Green Salad**
**Italian Oven Bread**
**Fresh Grapes and Biscotti**
(Butter Cookies)
**Sparkling Cider**

## PASTA WITH TOMATO SAUCE

(Serves 8-10)

3 large cans of Hunt's Special Tomato Sauce or 2 qts. canned tomatoes
3 6-oz. cans tomato paste
1 green pepper, halved or chopped
2 tsp. oregano
2 tsp. sweet basil
6 garlic cloves, minced or pressed
2 tsp. onion salt
1 bay leaf
  Dash of sugar
  Dash of lemon juice

1. Let all ingredients simmer a minimum of 1 hour or until green pepper is soft. The longer the sauce simmers, the more flavor the sauce will have.
2. May add mushrooms, onions, or pecan meatballs.
3. After simmering, before serving, remove halved green pepper and bay leaf.

Makes 2½ quarts.

# PASTA

(Serves 4)

1 8-oz. package spaghetti

Follow directions on package. Prepare just before serving. Makes 4 cups.

# PECAN MEATBALLS

(Serves 8-10)

1 8-oz. package cream cheese or Neufchâtel cheese, room temperature
4 large eggs*
1 large onion, chopped
2 cups soda crackers, crushed
1 cup pecans, chopped coarsely
1 tsp. sage
2 tsp. garlic powder

1. Cream together cream cheese and eggs.
2. Stir in remaining ingredients.
3. Let sit to thicken, form balls, and brown in lightly oiled pan, turning to avoid burning, or lightly oil cookie sheet and bake meatballs at 350 to 400° F and turn after 10 to 15 minutes. Bake approximately 30 minutes or until browned. Meatballs are great dipped in spaghetti sauce or simmered in mushroom soup gravy. May freeze meatballs for later use.

*Variations:* Tofu Pecan Meatballs
Replace eggs and cream cheese with 16 ounces of tofu (soft or regular firmness), mashed. If using regular firmness, blend in blender or food processor until smooth. Let sit in refrigerator to thicken. Continue with step 3.

Cottage Cheese Pecan Meatballs
You may also replace cream cheese in recipe with 8 ounces of cottage cheese blended until smooth.

Makes 15 to 20 medium-sized balls.

* This recipe contains one-half egg per serving.

# TOSSED GREEN SALAD

(Serves 4-6)

1 bunch leaf lettuce
2 tbsp. olive oil
2 tbsp. lemon juice
  Salt to taste
1 red onion, sliced
  Parmesan cheese

1. To avoid browning edges, break lettuce into bowl.
2. Add small amount of olive oil and lemon juice and salt to taste and toss, marinating the lettuce just before serving to avoid wilting.
3. Garnish with red onions, Parmesan cheese. Serve.

# FRESH GRAPES AND BISCOTTI

(BUTTER COOKIES)

Serve fresh grapes clusters in a basket. Can be used as an excellent centerpiece for your Italian dinner.

Serve Biscotti cookies on an attractive dessert plate (optional).

# SPARKLING CIDER

(Serves 4-6)

2 cups apple cider, chilled
2 cups diet lemon-lime carbonated beverage, chilled

Mix apple cider and carbonated beverage just before serving to preserve carbonation. Serve chilled or over ice cubes. Makes 4 cups.

NUTRITIONAL ANALYSIS FOR MENU

| | |
|---|---|
| Calories | 764 |
| Fat | 19g |
| Protein | 27g |
|    U.S. RDA | 59% |
| Cholesterol | 80mg |
| Sodium | 602mg |
| Carbohydrate | 122g |

# WEST COAST GARDEN DINNER

Boiled Artichokes With Dip
Creamy Scalloped Potatoes
Buttered-Chive Carrots
California Lettuce Salad
Oregon Blueberry Pie
Orange Soda Swizzle

## BOILED ARTICHOKES WITH DIP

4 medium artichokes
(1 per person)
Mayonnaise, low-fat if
desired, or garlic butter

(Serves 4)

1. When shopping for artichokes, look for plump, heavy globes and compact leaves. If bottom leaves snap when broken off, it is a sign of freshness.
2. To Cook: Remove discolored leaves and small leaves at base of artichoke. Trim off stem even with base. Using a serrated knife, cut the very tip off to remove spines. Snip off spines of remaining leaves with scissors. Rinse under cold water.
3. Artichokes should be cooked in large kettle. (May tie string around artichokes from top to bottom to hold leaves in place if desired.) For four medium artichokes heat 6 quarts of water, 2 tablespoons of lemon juice (to prevent discoloration). Add artichokes, stem down in water.
4. Heat to boiling, reduce heat. Simmer uncovered, rotating occasionally until leaves pull out easily and bottom is tender when pierced with knife, 30 to 40 minutes.
5. Carefully remove artichokes from water (use tongs or two large spoons); place upside down to drain.
6. To Serve: Remove string and place upright on plate. Accompany with small cup of low-fat mayonnaise or garlic butter if desired.
7. To Eat: Pluck leaves, one at a time. Dip base of leaf into dip or garlic butter. Turn leaf meaty side down and draw between teeth, scraping meaty portion with bottom teeth. Discard leaf on plate.
When all outer leaves have been removed, a center cone of small light-colored leaves covering the fuzzy center choke will be exposed. Pull or cut off cone of leaves. Slice off fuzzy choke with knife and fork; discard. Cut the remaining "heart" (the best part!) into bite-sized pieces and dip. Enjoy!

# CREAMY SCALLOPED POTATOES

6 medium potatoes
3 tbsp. margarine
3 tbsp. flour
1 tsp. salt
2½ cups skim milk*
1 small onion, finely chopped
1 tbsp. margarine

(Serves 4)
1. Wash and peel potatoes. Cut into thin slices.
2. Melt 3 tablespoons margarine in saucepan over low heat. Blend in flour and salt.
3. Remove from heat. Stir in milk. Heat to boiling, stirring constantly. Boil and stir 1 minute.
4. Arrange sliced potatoes in greased 2-quart casserole in three layers, alternating potatoes, onions, and white sauce. (May add cheese, if desired.)
5. Dot with 1 tablespoon margarine. Cover and cook at 350° F for 30 minutes. Uncover and cook until potatoes are tender, 60 to 70 minutes longer. Serve.

* May use any milk substitute—almond milk, soy milk, etc. See recipes in last chapter under variation recipes.

# BUTTERED-CHIVE CARROTS

1½ lb. fresh or frozen carrots
¼ cup margarine
¼ tsp. salt (optional)
1 tbsp. snipped chives

(Serves 4)
1. Scrape fresh carrots and remove ends.
2. Place carrots in 1 inch of boiling water. Cover and bring back to a boil. Turn heat to medium and cook until tender, approximately 20 minutes. Drain.
3. Heat margarine in 10-inch skillet until melted; add cooked carrots. Sprinkle with salt and chives. Heat, turning occasionally to coat with margarine.

# CALIFORNIA LETTUCE SALAD

1 small bunch Romaine lettuce, torn into pieces
2 tbsp. olive oil
1 medium zucchini, sliced
½ cup radishes, sliced
3 green onions, sliced
2 carrots, grated
1 tbsp. lemon juice
1 small garlic clove, crushed
Salt to taste (optional)
Slivered almonds

(Serves 6-8)
1. Toss Romaine lettuce and oil until leaves glisten.
2. Add remaining ingredients; toss. Garnish with slivered almonds.
3. Serve immediately to prevent lettuce from wilting.

# OREGON BLUEBERRY PIE

Blueberry Filling:
4 cups fresh or frozen blueberries
1 cup frozen grape juice concentrate, undiluted
1-1½ cups water
¼ cup quick-cooking tapioca
1½ tsp. vanilla
2 tsp. lemon juice

(Serves 8)
1. Wash and drain fresh blueberries. If using frozen blueberries, thaw and drain.
2. Mix grape juice concentrate, water, and tapioca in medium saucepan. Bring to a boil; remove from heat and let stand 15 to 20 minutes.
3. Return to heat and bring to boil; simmer approximately 5 to 10 minutes, stirring constantly.
4. Stir blueberries into thickened sauce. Remove from heat; stir in vanilla and lemon juice; cool.
5. Pour into baked piecrust. (Recipe following.)
6. Refrigerate 2-4 hours before serving.

*Variations:* May use blackberries or boysenberries in place of blueberries.

# PIECRUST

Food Processor Directions:

6 tbsp. cold margarine or
  vegetable shortening
1¼ cups flour—not packed
¼ tsp. salt
4 tbsp. water

1. Place cold margarine or vegetable shortening, flour and salt in processor with chop blade and process with short pulses, cutting shortening into flour.
2. Add water all at once and process until dough forms a ball. (Divide into 2 balls for double recipe, p.101.
3. Place on floured surface and roll into circle about 2 inches larger than pie pan.
4. Press into bottom of pan. Prick bottom and sides of crust with fork to prevent air bubbles when baking.
5. Bake at 350° F until lightly brown, 8 to 10 minutes.

*Handmade Piecrust Directions*:

1. Place vegetable shortening, flour, and salt in bowl. Cut shortening into dry ingredients until fine and crumbly.
2. Sprinkle in water, 1 teaspoon at a time, tossing lightly with fork until flour is moistened and pastry almost cleans the side of bowl. Gather pastry into a ball. Continue with food-processor steps 3 to 5.

# ORANGE SODA SWIZZLE

6 oz. frozen orange juice
  concentrate, thawed
2 cups club soda, chilled

(Serves 4)

Mix chilled club soda and frozen orange juice concentrate, thawed. Serve immediately.
Makes 3 cups.

NUTRITIONAL ANALYSIS FOR MENU

Calories.................................................................832
Fat ........................................................................31g
Protein ...............................................................23.7g
    U.S. RDA .......................................................41%
Cholesterol.......................................................2.08mg
Sodium ..........................................................884.5mg
Carbohydrate.......................................................133g

# SPECIAL OCCASIONS

♦ Mother's Day Brunch
♦ Thanksgiving Dinner—Hold the Turkey
♦ Afternoon Garden Party

# MOTHER'S DAY BRUNCH

**Crepes With Cheese Blintz Filling**
**Toppings: Raspberry Sauce**
**Blueberry Sauce**
**Sparkling Fruit Compote**
**Banana-Blueberry Muffins**
**Blushing Orange Frost Punch**

## CREPES WITH CHEESE BLINTZ FILLING

### CREPES
1½ cups all-purpose flour
1 tbsp. sugar (optional)
½ tsp. salt
2 cups milk, skim*
2 eggs†
2 tbsp. melted margarine
½ tsp. vanilla

(Serves 12)

1. Mix together flour, sugar, and salt. Stir in remaining ingredients.
2. Beat with hand mixer until smooth.
3. Melt small amount of margarine in 6" to 8" nonstick skillet.
4. Pour scant ¼ cup of batter into skillet; immediately rotate skillet until thin film covers bottom of skillet.
5. Cook just until light brown. Run wide spatula around edge to loosen. Remove crepe and continue, stacking crepes with waxed paper between each one. Keep covered. Serve immediately, or freeze until needed.

*May use any milk substitute—almond milk, soy milk, etc. See recipes in last chapter under variation recipes.

† This recipe contains one-sixth of an egg per serving.

## CHEESE BLINTZ FILLING

- 2 cups small-curd cottage cheese, blended
- 1 tbsp. lemon juice
- 1 tbsp. honey
- ½ tsp. vanilla
- ½ cup sour cream (optional)

1. Mix all ingredients together well.
2. Spread 2 tablespoonful on each crepe.
3. Roll up like a jelly roll, or fold both sides toward center.
4. Serve hot with or without toppings.

Makes 2½ to 3 cups.

# BERRY SAUCE

- 4 cups raspberries or blueberries, unsweetened, fresh or frozen
- 1 cup frozen apple juice concentrate if using raspberries; or 1 cup frozen grape juice concentrate if using blueberries
- 1-1½ cups water
- ¼ cup quick-cooking tapioca
- 1½ tsp. vanilla or coconut flavoring
- 2 tsp. lemon juice
  Dash of salt

1. Wash and drain fresh berries. If using frozen berries, drain berries while thawing.
2. Mix juice concentrate, water, and tapioca in medium saucepan. Bring to a boil; remove from heat and let stand 15 to 20 minutes.
3. Return to heat and bring to boil; simmer approximately 5 to 10 minutes, stirring constantly, until tapioca granules are clear and soft.
4. Stir berries into thickened sauce.
5. Remove from heat; add flavoring, lemon juice, and salt.
6. Cool and serve over crepes.

Makes 3 cups.

*Variations*: Use blackberries or boysenberries in place of blueberries. Use strawberries in place of raspberries. May use as a filling for a pie or as topping for pancakes, waffles, or toast.

# SPARKLING FRUIT COMPOTE

- 3 medium peaches
- 2 cups sliced strawberries
- 2 cups red seedless grapes
- 2 cups melon balls
- 3 medium bananas
- 1 bottle pink sparkling grape juice, chilled

(Serves 8-10)

1. Slice peaches into bowl. Top peach slices with strawberries, red grapes, and melon balls.
2. Cover and refrigerate.
3. Just before serving, slice bananas into fruit mixture.
4. Pour sparkling grape juice on fruit and lightly toss. Serve immediately.

**OPTION:** *Sparkling Grape Juice*: Mix 12 ounces of chilled grape juice with 12 ounces of chilled lemon-lime carbonated beverage.

# BANANA-BLUEBERRY MUFFINS

(Serves 12)

2 eggs, separated*
2/3 cup milk†
1/3 cup vegetable oil
1 ripe banana, mashed
2 cups flour, whole wheat or white
2 tsp. baking soda** (optional)
1/3 cup sugar
2 tsp. cinnamon
1½ cups blueberries, fresh or frozen

1. Mix 1 egg yolk (1 yolk discarded); add milk, oil, and mashed banana.
2. Stir in flour, soda, sugar, and cinnamon.
3. Fold in blueberries.
4. Beat egg whites until stiff, but not dry; quickly and carefully fold into the batter.
5. Spray muffin tins with Pam or lightly grease. Fill cups about three quarters full.
6. Bake in preheated oven at 350° F for 10 to 12 minutes or until golden brown. Immediately remove from pan.

These muffins freeze well.

\* This recipe contains one-eighth egg per serving.
† May use any milk substitute—almond milk, soy milk, etc. See recipes in last chapter under variation recipes.
\*\* Baking soda may be omitted in this recipe. However, muffins will not be as light without it.

# BLUSHING ORANGE FROST PUNCH

(Serves 12)

2 bananas, chunked
1½ qt. orange juice
2 cups frozen strawberries
24 oz. or 4 cups diet lemon-lime carbonated beverage (optional)

1. In blender, to bananas add 1 cup of orange juice or enough juice to blend bananas smooth. Pour into 3½ to 4-quart container.
2. Blend strawberries with 1 to 2 cups of orange juice until smooth, and pour into banana mixture.
3. Add remaining orange juice, and mix. Chill until serving time.
4. Add carbonated beverage just before serving.

Makes approximately 3 quarts.

NUTRITIONAL ANALYSIS FOR MENU

| | |
|---|---|
| Calories | 584 |
| Fat | 11.5g |
| Protein | 15.6g |
| U.S. RDA | 34% |
| Cholesterol | 60mg |
| Sodium | 407mg |
| Carbohydrate | 108g |

# THANKSGIVING DINNER—HOLD THE TURKEY

**Suggested Menu**
Cottage Cheese Croquettes With Gravy
Mashed Potatoes
Yams in Orange Juice Marinade
Fresh Steamed Broccoli
Cranberry-Orange Relish
Dinner Rolls ♦ Bubbly Apple Drink
Apple Pie ♦ Hot Spiced Orange Tea

## COTTAGE CHEESE CROQUETTES WITH GRAVY

¼-½ cup minced onion
1 tbsp. oil
2 cups low-fat cottage cheese*
3 eggs, beaten*†
1 cup soft whole-wheat bread crumbs
1¾ cups dry bread crumbs
¼ cup nuts, chopped (optional)
1 tbsp. chicken seasoning (McKays or any brand without animal fat)
2 tbsp. yeast flakes (optional)
½ tsp. sage
½ tsp. thyme
½ tsp. salt or to taste

(Serves 8)

1. Sauté onion in oil until soft.
2. Combine all remaining ingredients with sautéed onion in medium-size mixing bowl.
3. Place mixture in refrigerator to firm for approximately 1 hour. (May leave overnight if desired.)
4. Form into croquettes and place into oiled baking dish. Place in 350° F oven until croquettes are brown.
5. Cover browned croquettes with gravy (recipe following) and bake at 350° F for 20 to 30 minutes or until the centers are thoroughly done.

*Variations: Low-fat Tofu Croquettes*
Replace eggs and cottage cheese with one 1-pound regular firmness tofu, blended until smooth. This makes an excellent croquette with little change in flavor.
*† This recipe contains one-third egg per serving.

# CHICKEN SEASONED GRAVY

¼-½ cup onion, chopped (optional)
4 tbsp. vegetable oil
7 tbsp. flour
3 cups water
1-2 tbsp. chicken seasoning (McKay's or any brand without animal fat)
Garlic salt to taste

(Serves 12-16)

1. Sauté onions in oil (if onion is desired) until tender. Turn heat to medium-low.
2. Whisk flour into hot oil, adding 2 tablespoons at a time, wisking with each addition until smooth.
3. Add water 1 cup at a time, whisking briefly with each addition until smooth. You may need to add more water as gravy simmers if you desire a thinner consistency.
4. Add chicken seasoning to taste, and garlic salt if desired. Serve.

# YAMS IN ORANGE JUICE MARINADE

2 lb. yams (about 6 medium)
½ cup orange juice
½ cup apricot nectar
⅓ cup honey and molasses combined (to desired sweetness)
1 tbsp. cornstarch
1 tsp. salt
¼ tsp. grated orange peel

(Serves 4-6)

1. Wash yams; do not peel.
2. Place yams in pan and cover with water.* Cover and heat to boiling. Turn heat to medium and cook until tender, 30 to 35 minutes; drain.
3. Slip off skins after yams cool enough to touch. Cut yams crosswise into half-inch circles. Place in 1½- to 2-quart covered baking dish.
4. In saucepan, combine and heat orange juice, molasses, and honey. To prevent lumps from forming, dissolve cornstarch in a few tablespoons of water before adding to heated orange juice mixture. Whisk until thickened and smooth. Stir in salt and orange peel.
5. Pour orange juice marinade over yams and bake at 350° F. for one hour, basting with orange juice marinade occasionally. Serve.

# APPLE PIE

(Serves 8-10)

1 6-oz. can frozen unsweetened apple juice concentrate, thawed
2 tbsp. cornstarch
1 tbsp. margarine
1 tsp. cinnamon
1 tsp. vanilla extract
6 medium-size tart apples,
   peeled, cored, and sliced
   Pastry (recipe follow-
     ing)

1. Combine apple juice concentrate and cornstarch in a medium saucepan, stirring well. Cook over medium heat until thickened and bubbly.
2. Stir in margarine, cinnamon, and vanilla. Add apples; toss well to coat. Pour into pastry-lined pie plate.
3. Cover with top crust.(Slit to allow steam to escape). Trim edge around pie pan, leaving half-inch overlap. Seal top with bottom crust. Flute edge.
4. Cover edge with strips of aluminum foil; remove foil during last 15 minutes of baking. Bake at 425° F until crust is brown and juice begins to bubble through slits in crust, 40 to 50 minutes.

## Double Crust

¾ cup cold margarine or
   vegetable shortening
2½ cups flour (do not pack)
½ tsp. salt
½ cup water

# PASTRY

**Food Processor and Handmade Piecrust Directions:**
Follow procedure, page 92.

# HOT SPICED ORANGE TEA

4 cups boiling water
4 tsp. caffein-free orange tea
   (May use 4 tea bags)
6 whole cloves
½ tsp. dried orange peel
⅛ tsp. ground cinnamon

(Serves 4-6)

1. Pour boiling water over tea, cloves, orange peel, and cinnamon in heat-proof container.
2. Cover and let stand until tea is desired strength, 3 to 5 minutes. Stir and strain. Serve with dessert.

NUTRITIONAL ANALYSIS FOR MENU

Calories .................................................................1117
Fat ...........................................................................41g
Protein ..................................................................38.1g
     U.S. RDA ............................................................78%
Cholesterol.........................................................104mg
Sodium .............................................................1548mg
Carbohydrate.......................................................197g

# AFTERNOON GARDEN PARTY

Lemon-Chive Red Potato Nibbles
Stuffed Mushrooms
Fresh Vegetable Platter With Spinach Dip
Wheat Thins With Raspberry and Cheese
Sparkling Cranberry Punch With Citrus Ice Ring

## LEMON-CHIVE RED POTATO NIBBLES

(Serves 4)

1½ lb. new red potatoes
    (10 to 12 small)
  3 tbsp. margarine
  1 tbsp. lemon juice
3-4 tsp. snipped chives
  ½ tsp. salt
  ¼ tsp. garlic powder
    (optional)
    Dash of nutmeg

1. To prepare potatoes, wash lightly and leave whole. If small new red potatoes are not available, you may use larger red potatoes and cut in 1½-inch chunks. New red potatoes are the most tender and have great flavor.
2. Place potatoes in 1 inch of water. Cover and heat to boiling, then turn temperature to medium and steam until potatoes are tender, 20 to 25 minutes. Drain.

**To Microwave:** Prick potatoes with fork to allow steam to escape. In casserole dish, place potatoes with ½-inch water and cover. Cook on high 10 minutes, turn potatoes and cook approximately 5 minutes longer or until tender. Let stand one minute and drain.

3. Heat margarine, lemon juice, chives, salt, and nutmeg just to boiling. (Garlic powder is a nice addition to this sauce.)
4. Turn hot potatoes into serving dish; pour lemon-chive butter over potatoes and lightly toss. To prevent butter from soaking into potatoes, serve immediately after tossing potatoes with butter mixture.

# STUFFED MUSHROOMS

(Serves 10-12)

8 oz. fresh mushrooms
1 tbsp. chopped green onion
2 tbsp. chopped mushroom
    tips
1 tbsp. margarine
2 tbsp. bread crumbs
2 tbsp. sour cream*
2 tbsp. grated mozzarella,
    Parmesan, or other
    cheese (optional)

1. Wash mushrooms. Cut stems from mushrooms and set aside to use for 2 tablespoons of chopped mushroom tips.
2. Sauté green onions and mushroom tips in margarine until tender. Remove from heat.
3. Stir bread crumbs and sour cream into sauté mixture.
4. Fill mushroom caps with stuffing mixture; place mushrooms, filled sides up, on cookie sheet. Sprinkle tops of mushrooms with grated cheese if desired.
5. Broil for 3 to 5 minutes or until browned. Serve immediately after removing from oven.

\* See variations for sour cream in last chapter.

# FRESH VEGETABLE PLATTER WITH SPINACH DIP

(Serves 10-12)

1 cup broccoli flowerets
1 cup cauliflower flowerets
1 cup carrot sticks
1 cup celery sticks
1 cup cucumber circles
1 cup radish roses
1 cup cherry tomatoes with
    stems
10 green onions
    Lettuce leaves (or any com-
    bination of vegetables)

1. Wash vegetables.
2. Prepare broccoli and cauliflower flowerets by cutting off thick stems and breaking flowerets off by hand.
3. Remove ends of carrots, peel, and cut into 4- to 6-inch sticks.
4. Cut off bottom stem of celery, break off each stalk, and cut into 4- to 6-inch sticks.
5. Remove ends of cucumber, and peel (optional). Cut into circle slices.
6. Remove stem and root ends from large radishes. Cut thin petals around radishes. Chill in bowl of ice and water until crisp and petals open.
7. Remove roots and loose layers of skin from green onions. Cut off top few inches of green to remove brown ends. For a fancier touch, you may cut thin slices down the

green part of the onion, making a lacy ribbon look. Soak in ice water until serving.

8. If more convenient, you may prepare vegetables 1 day ahead and store in water and airtight containers. If preparing a few hours ahead, you may simply place a damp towel over arranged platter and refrigerate.

9. Place lettuce leaves on platter. Arrange vegetables attractively on leaves. Serve with Spinach Dip.

# SPINACH DIP

10 oz. frozen spinach, chopped
1 pkg. Knorr's Vegetable Soup and Recipe Mix (any other dry vegetable or onion soup mix if Knorr's is not available)
1½ cups sour cream*
1 cup mayonnaise†
8 oz. water chestnuts, chopped
3 green onions with tops, chopped

(serves 40)
1. Thaw spinach and squeeze until liquid has drained.
2. Stir spinach together with remaining ingredients.
3. Cover and refrigerate a minimum of 2 hours before serving. Stir again just before serving.

Makes 4½ to 5 cups. Nutrition information based on 2 tablespoon servings.

* See variations for sour cream in last chapter.
† May also replace mayonnaise with a sour cream variation.

# WHEAT THINS WITH RASPBERRY JAM AND CHEESE

1 small box Wheat Thins or Homemade Wheat Thins (recipe, p. 38)
1 8-oz package Neufchâtel cheese, softened
1-1½ cups raspberry jam (recipe following, or jam of choice)

(Serves 10-12)
1. On platter, spread softened Neufchâtel cheese evenly to outside edge.
2. Spread jam evenly over Neufchâtel to within 1 inch of edge.
3. Place crackers in cheese, making a circle around outside edge.
4. Serve immediately. To prepare ahead, simply leave crackers off until serving time and cover cheese and jam on platter with Saran Wrap and refrigerate.

# RASPBERRY JAM

2½ tbsp. cornstarch
1⅛ cups apple juice
1⅛ cups raspberries, fresh or frozen, thawed
½ tbsp. honey
⅛ tsp. lemon juice

1. In saucepan, dissolve cornstarch in chilled apple juice. Bring mixture to a boil and continue to boil 1 minute over medium heat, stirring constantly as mixture thickens.
2. Add remaining ingredients. May add more honey to acquire desired sweetness.
3. Cook 30 seconds. Chill.
Makes 2½ cups.

# SPARKLING CRANBERRY PUNCH

4 cups cranberry juice
2 cups sugar-free carbonated lemon-lime beverage

(Serves 8-10)
1. Mix carbonated beverage into juice just before serving, to preserve carbonation.
2. Serve in punch bowl with citrus ice ring.
Makes 6 cups.

# CITRUS ICE RING

2 oranges, sliced thinly in circles
2 limes, sliced thinly in circles
7-9 strawberries with stems

1. Arrange citrus slices and strawberries in an attractive design in a 6- to 6½-cup ring mold. Pour water into mold to partially cover fruit; freeze.
2. When frozen, add water to fill mold three-quarters full; freeze.
3. At serving time, unmold and float fruit side up in punch bowl.

NUTRITIONAL ANALYSIS FOR MENU

Calories.................................................................................................606
Fat .......................................................................................................28g
Protein................................................................................................12.9g
    U.S. RDA.....................................................................................28%
Cholesterol.......................................................................................32.6mg
Sodium...............................................................................................719mg
Carbohydrate.........................................................................................76g

# VARIATIONS

♦Milk
♦Sour Cream

# MILK VARIATIONS

**Simple Soymilk**
**Instant Soymilk**
**Rice-Cashew Milk**
**Almond Milk**

## SIMPLE SOYMILK

2 cups soybeans
2 qts. water

1. Soak soybeans overnight in water.
2. The next day, heat beans in same water, bringing to a full boil.
3. Lower heat and simmer five minutes longer.
4. Pour off foamy liquid and add cold water to stop the cooking process.
5. Whiz 3 cups at a time on liquify cycle of blender, adding water until liquid is the proper consistency of milk.
6. To resemble milk more, strain soymilk by pouring it through cheesecloth-lined sieve. Lift cloth out when finished and squeeze any remaining liquid out. If using soymilk for cooking, there is no need to strain it.

# INSTANT SOYMILK

Instant soymilk powder is available at health food stores and some grocery stores. All you need to do is mix water and the soymilk powder in blender and serve.

# RICE-CASHEW MILK

⅔ cup hot rice
½ cup cashews
1 tsp. vanilla
½ tsp. salt
3-4 softened dates or 3 to 4 tsp. honey
3 cups water
1 banana (optional)

(Serves 8-10)
1. Whiz together all ingredients until smooth.
2. Chill and serve.
Makes approximately 4½ cups.

NOTE: If using in creamy gravy or soups, use less water to give a thicker, creamier texture. Add 1 cup of water at a time to reach desired texture.

# ALMOND MILK

¾ cup almonds (or cashews), blanched lightly
1 tbsp. minced dates or 2 tbsp. honey
¼ cup sesame seeds
5 cups water
¼ tsp. salt
1 tsp. vanilla

1. Place almonds, dates, sesame seeds, and a small amount of water in blender.
2. Whiz until completely blended. Add remaining water and other ingredients.
3. Strain in cheesecloth-lined sieve—squeezing out remaining milk from cheesecloth. Chill before serving.

Great over cereals, for drinking, and for replacing milk in recipes.

# SOUR CREAM VARIATIONS

**Cottage Cheese Sour Cream**
**Yogurt Sour Cream**
**Cottage Cheese-Yogurt Sour Cream**

## COTTAGE CHEESE SOUR CREAM

1. Place cottage cheese in blender. Blend until cottage cheese is velvety smooth. Carefully push cheese down from sides of blender with spatula while processing.
2. Chill; it is ready to replace sour cream in recipes.

NOTE: Use low-fat cottage cheese for even fewer calories.

## YOGURT SOUR CREAM

Use plain low-fat yogurt in place of sour cream in recipes.

## COTTAGE CHEESE-YOGURT SOUR CREAM

Mix cottage cheese sour cream with yogurt, using equal parts of each. The yogurt gives the cottage cheese a more sour taste, better resembling sour cream.

NOTE: Again, using low-fat cottage cheese and low-fat yogurt reduces calories even more.

# INDEX